Remember the 80's, Jersey Girl

Copyright © 2017 Donna M. Fox, Jersey Girl Publications LLC
Written by Donna M. Fox
Illustrations by Sue Gioulis and Maria Lynskey
Graphic Design by Steve Lingle

Printed by IngramSpark

ISBN-13: 978-0-692-96563-4

Remember the 80's, Jersey Girl

An Illustrated Children's Book

Jersey Girl Publications

Dedicated to the
Cherokee High School Class of 1990
"Never Say Goodbye"

and to my
Aunt Jean,
who lives life to
the fullest in
every decade

Growing up in the 80's was one of the
happiest times in Jersey Girl's life!

The hair was BIG,

and the love for music was even bigger. Hours were spent *simply listening*... surrounded by Teen Beat posters, stuffed animals, stereo speakers, and countless stacks of cassettes and albums.

Every day, Jersey Girl and her neighbors
played outside in the fresh air

until 5pm when their moms called them
all home for dinner.

The houses were decorated with
colorful velour wallpaper,

shag rugs, flowery slip covers,
and shimmery curtains.

On rainy days, the boys would build forts, play
with train sets and Matchbox cars, or play Atari
and Nintendo on the television in the family
room... PacMan, Asteroids, and Donkey Kong...
while the girls played Spirograph, Fashion Plates,
Colorforms, dollhouses, Barbies, school, and
dress up in the basement.

For entertainment, the VCR was the newest way to watch movies at home. Families would rent tapes on stormy nights from Blockbuster or the local video store in town and gather around the TV, cozy with blankets and freshly microwaved popcorn.

Weekends were for rollerskating at the local rink to the music of the time. When the floor was cleared for a slow song, everyone went to the side and washed their wheels, waiting hopefully to skate with a partner to a dreamy 80's love song like "Can't Fight This Feeling" or "I Want To Know What Love Is."

A birthday party at the roller rink was a
dream come true for this Jersey Girl!

The 80's were about romance... notes in lockers from first boyfriends, waiting by the radio at night to hear and record dedicated love songs, and dancing on Friday nights in the church or school cafeteria. Lasting memories were formed from these experiences of bonding and connection.

All week long, Jersey Girl and her friends looked forward to going out as a group to Friendly's after an event and *talking* and *laughing*... laughing so hard together, and never being distracted by a single thing. This was a GIFT they didn't realize at the time, and it was the purest form of enjoying each other's company.

If a friend was absent from school and missing from the lunch table, one quarter and a payphone was all Jersey Girl needed to call the friend at home and see how he or she was feeling. To make the call, she had to know the seven digit phone number or refer to her phone book. Jersey Girl also used this payphone to call and ask a parent for a ride home after a school dance or meeting.

Receiving that long-awaited call on the house phone, finding a blinking light on the answering machine, or being surprised with a letter in the mailbox was something to look forward to at the end of the school day. The sound of the telephone ringing at the house was exciting since there was *no way* of knowing who was calling!

The patience gained from all of the hopeful anticipation during this decade taught Jersey Girl the value of TRULY WAITING for anything that was worthwhile... especially the simplest and sweetest things... like listening closely to the radio on a snowy morning for her school's number in hopes of a snow day, or waiting to wear her new red boots for the annual picture with Santa.

In this spirit, old fashioned cameras with film were used to preserve her memories from the 80's. Jersey Girl waited for days to see these memories in print, and she is so THANKFUL that she did.

Epilogue

This brief collection of memories simply touches upon some of the highlights of our generation growing up. It is meant to be a catalyst for discussion with your youngest loved ones. There are so many 80's memories, I begin the list here... add to it as you wish, and share the connection with this time period for years to come. We must never forget the days before technology, as we were the last to experience childhood during this sacred time of waiting for gratification and truly connecting with others without distraction. My wish is that we carry the feelings, spirit, values, and music forward so our children and theirs will have a piece of the 80's with them always.

Donna M. Lynskey
Cherokee High School
Class of 1990

Remember the 80's

Going to the movies cost $5.00 and mailing a letter cost $.25
Braces that you could see
Prince
Phil Collins
Michael Jackson
Donna Summer
Whitney Houston
Madonna
Journey
George Michael
The Bee Gees
Chicago
Culture Club
867-5309 and Jesse's Girl
YMCA
Boombox and Walkman
Legwarmers and Parachute Pants
Fashion Bug and Kmart
White Keds and Jellies
Scrunchies and Streamer Barrettes
Flourescent clothes and bracelets
Gold jewelry with names or initials and half of a heart charms
One can of hairspray per week
Rave home perms in the laundry room
Typewriters, Typing Class, and Cursive Writing
Textbooks wrapped in brown paper bags
Sweet Valley High Books
Beverly Cleary and Judy Blume
Cats in the Cradle and Chinese Jump Rope
Rubik's Cube and Missing Link
Smurfs, Cabbage Patch Dolls, and Strawberry Shortcake
Copying a newspaper comic strip onto Silly Putty
Stories on record
Walking to school
Eating dinner as a family
Dot candy and candy bracelets
Brady Bunch and Little House on the Prairie
Gilligan's Island and The Price is Right
Stamp Collection and Scratch and Sniff Sticker Collection
2 keys for every car
Hot metal seat belts in the summer
Chevrolet Caprice Classic, Monte Carlo, and Station Wagon
Awesome and grody
Trapper Keeper
Card Catalogs and Encyclopedias
Footloose and The Outsiders
Patrick Swayze and Tom Cruise
Sylvester Stallone
Back to the Future and Ghostbusters
ET, MTV, TAB
Collectible glasses from McDonald's with characters on them
Knew where your friends were by the bikes on the lawn

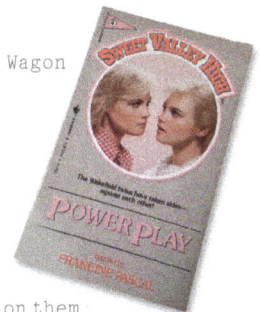

Share your memories.

Use this space to record your own stream of memories
from the 80's or to illustrate your favorite
Remember the 80's, Jersey Girl moments.

We would love for you to share these or other special
80's moments online at www.jerseygirlpublications.com.

About Us

Illustrator

Sue Gioulis has loved to draw since her childhood days in Westfield, New Jersey, and her first formal illustration was done for *Parents Magazine Press* in 1972. Her formal training was completed at the Ringling School of Art in Sarasota, Florida. She is a member of the Manasquan River Group of Artists and displays her work at the Main Avenue Galleria in Ocean Grove, New Jersey. Sue has illustrated several children's books including Donna's first, *Jersey Girl*, and has most recently recreated memories from the 1980's in *Remember the 80's, Jersey Girl*. Using photographs of scenes, people, and outfits of the time, Donna and Sue collaborated on each piece of art to create a feeling of warmth and connection with this time period. Sue enjoys art projects and her life at the Jersey Shore surrounded by husband, children, and grandchildren.

Author

Jersey Girl Donna Fox lovingly recalls her hometown of Marlton, NJ as she reminisces in *Remember the 80's, Jersey Girl*. The photos, memorabilia, and artwork in this memoir represent relatable moments in her life from 1978-1992. This is the second book in the collection of Jersey Girl children's books that Donna is creating in hopes that her works will spark discussion and memories in her readers, and that they will see a piece of themselves and their past in the character of Jersey Girl... no matter which state they are from. Both Jersey Girl books have a common thread of GIFTS and THANKFULNESS, and both give back to our communities by benefiting a local related charity. Donna was thrilled to work with Steve Lingle, her Cherokee High School homeroom friend, as her graphic designer for this book, and she is thankful to her brother, Danny, for living the 80's right by her side.

Illustrator

The proud mother of Donna, Maria Lynskey is responsible for capturing nearly all of the moments on film in *Remember the 80's, Jersey Girl*. Maria enjoyed photographing her son and daughter as they grew, and she knew the value of preserving a memory for them to look back on years later. Maria has also recently illustrated *Jersey Girl*, a book for which she created two stunning oil paintings and shared her valuable vintage photos from the 1970's of her family at the Jersey Shore. Donna's childhood silhouette trademark representing Jersey Girl Publications is so meaningful as that, too, was an oil painting done by her mother. Maria feels that it is truly a blessing to know that the upbringing she and her husband, Tom, provided for their children is sincerely appreciated today. She is so thankful for her two beautiful grandchildren, two gifts given to her by Donna and Dan.

www.ingramcontent.com/pod-product-compliance
Lightning Source LLC
Chambersburg PA
CBHW040244100426
42811CB00011B/1150